ASPECTS OF ROM

ROMAN RELIGION

MICHAEL MASSEY
Southgate School, London

88

LONGMAN

1: EARLY BELIEFS

A curse tablet showing a devil-like figure and containing a curse written in nonsense words.

Mosaic design of the 'evil eye', which is meant to ward off bad luck.

Ever since men first walked on the earth, they have tried to understand the world around them. They have tried to answer such questions as: How does life begin? What makes crops grow? Why does it rain? Where do people go when they die? The more they thought about these questions, the more they believed that there were unseen forces or spirits which controlled everything around them. Sometimes these forces seemed to make things turn out well; at other times they brought disaster.

Not knowing what these forces would do next, early man did his best to control them in various ways. By repeating magic spells and working magic charms he hoped to get the good spirits on his side and to prevent the bad spirits doing him harm. In this way he tried to make the rain-spirit send rain to help the crops to grow, and made up spells to keep away the mildew-spirits which might ruin the harvest. Some people think that the cave paintings found in very old caves were really magic spells to help the stone-age cave-dwellers do well in their hunting.

Many of our superstitions are based on early ideas of magic and the worship of spirits. For example, even today people cross their fingers to bring good-luck. What they are really doing is tying a knot in their fingers so that 'bad' magic cannot reach and affect them.

This relief carving shows a procession on its way to make a sacrifice of a bull, a sheep and a boar.

Spirits

To understand how Roman religion developed we must go back to the eighth century B.C., long before Rome became a great city, when the Romans were a farming community, settled on the banks of the river Tiber.

The early Romans thought that such things as harvests, success in trade and war, and health were controlled by spirits. They called these spirits **numina.** The farmers thought there were spirits in the fields, springs, rivers, trees and crops. As the spirits were a part of everything the farmer did, he had to make sure that he could keep them on his side so that they would be good to him. To do this he would make offerings of wine or food and, on special festival days, he would kill an animal and offer its body to the spirits. This was known as a **sacrifice.**

The Romans often referred to the worship of spirits in their writings. The poet Horace was especially grateful for the cool water of a spring near his farm and he wrote the following poem, which shows us how a religious Roman would show his gratitude to the spirit of the spring:

Spring of Bandusia, clearer than crystal, you deserve an offering of best wine and garlands of flowers; and tomorrow a young goat will be killed and offered to the spirit of your waters . . .
The hottest of days cannot change the coolness of your stream, where bulls, tired from the plough, and wandering sheep find refreshment.

Horace *Odes* 3.13

The spring of Bandusia, near Horace's farm at Tivoli.

There were certain times when the farmer had to pay special attention to the spirits of the countryside: after buying a new farm, for example:

When the head of the household arrives at the farmhouse, he should make an immediate tour of the farm, as soon as he has paid his respects to the spirits of the household.

Cato *On Agriculture* 2.1

Or when taking care of oxen:

Make offerings as follows to keep your oxen in good health. Make the following offerings to Mars Silvanus in the wood during the day: three pounds of wheat, four and a half of lard, four and a half of meat and three pints of wine. Either a slave or a free man may offer this sacrifice. After the sacrifice, eat it at once and in the same place. No woman should be present at this sacrifice or see how it is done.

Cato *On Agriculture* 83.1

The Romans thought either that the presence of women would affect the success of the sacrifice or that religious ceremonies like this should only be carried out by men: in this way their power over women could be maintained.

Although the Romans gradually changed their ideas about religion as they grew more used to city life, they still kept up many of the old beliefs about spirits.

The Romans used the word **religio** to describe the feeling of relationship which they thought ought to exist between men and spirits. Our word 'religion' comes from this Latin word and means binding oneself to a spirit or god.

This small pig, found at Herculaneum in Italy, is supposed to be a likeness of the Spirit of the pig. (Height 11.5cm)

QUESTIONS

1 What kinds of spirits or unseen forces did the early Romans believe existed? (pages 2 and 3)

2 How did the Romans try to control these spirits? (page 2)

3 What did a Roman farmer do when he visited his new farm, according to Cato? (page 5)

4 To whom does Cato say the farmer should offer a sacrifice to keep his oxen in good health? (page 5)

5 Who was forbidden to be present at such a ceremony? Why was this so? (page 5)

6 How does Horace say he will show his gratitude to the Spring of Bandusia? (page 4)

7 What is a sacrifice? (page 3)

THINGS TO DO

1 Make a list of the sorts of things which country people would think were due to the work of spirits. For example, they might wonder what caused the lightning to flash or the rain to fall.

2 Try to find out if any of the modern superstitions you know are based on early magic.

A *Lararium*, or shrine of the household spirits. (This is a model and is about 2m high.)

2: FAMILY RELIGION

Statuette of a *Lar*, or spirit of the Household. (About 20cm high)

Private religion played an important part in Roman family life. All the main events in a person's life were celebrated by religious ceremonies, and the day-to-day life of the family was governed by certain religious beliefs and rituals.

The centre of a Roman's life was his household. He believed that it was protected by spirits and that the happiness and success of his house and family depended on the goodwill of these spirits.

There were two main groups: the **lares** and the **penates.** The *Lares* were the spirits of the family's ancestors and they protected the entire household. Every house had a shrine, called a **lararium,** which stood in a corner of the main living room. It was like a small cupboard and statues of the *lares* were kept in it. The top was shaped like the roof of a temple, and there were sometimes pictures of the *lares* painted on the front. The *penates* were the spirits who protected the larder or store-house of the family. It was important to worship them so that the family always had enough to eat.

The head of the family was called the **paterfamilias,** and it was his duty to organise the family worship. He made offerings of wine and incense to the *lares* and *penates* every day on behalf of his family.

In a world where the making of fire was a difficult business, the family's hearth was very important for providing warmth, light and a means of cooking food. The Romans called the flame of the hearth **vesta.** The *paterfamilias* prayed to the *vesta* before the main meal each day, and, during the meal, some of the food was thrown into the flames as an offering.

There were many other spirits connected with the household and the Romans gave names to them all. For example, they called the spirit of the doorway **Janus.** But the Romans thought that a door also needed a spirit to open it (**Janus Patulcius**) and a spirit to close it (**Janus Clusivius**). (Later Christian writers made fun of all the spirits which the Romans worshipped.)

The *paterfamilias* had to remember all of these spirits, and he had to make sure that he performed the rituals and said the prayers correctly. If he made a mistake or forgot a spirit, the family or household might be harmed in some way.

This is a likeness of Janus from a coin. He faces both ways because he is a god of beginnings and endings as well as of doors, which have an inside and an outside.

Statue of a *Paterfamilias.* He is holding the portrait masks of two of his ancestors. (About life-size)

A bulla, worn round a child's neck to keep away evil spirits. (About 10cm high)

Childhood

In Roman times women often died while giving birth. If a woman was about to have a baby, her husband offered prayers to the goddess **Juno Lucina.** People believed that this goddess would protect the mother during such a dangerous time. The name Lucina means 'the bringer of light' – a good name for a goddess who brought happiness to many families.

Nine days after its birth (eight for a girl) the child was given its first name, and a magic charm called a **bulla** was hung round its neck to protect it from evil spirits which might bring disease or death. Boys wore this charm until the age of about sixteen, when they officially became men. At a special ceremony the boy dedicated his *bulla* to the *lares* of the household. A girl would dedicate her *bulla* to the *lares* on the night before her wedding. The dedication ceremony consisted of a prayer of thanksgiving to the *lares* for having protected the children during their early life.

Marriage

Marriage, too, involved religious rituals. The bride, dressed in a white tunic and orange veil, waited for the arrival of the groom in her father's house. A pig or a sheep was sacrificed to the gods and an official, called an **Auspex,** cut open the animal and inspected its insides. By noting the colour, shape and size of the insides he could tell whether the gods favoured the marriage. If they did not he had the power to stop the marriage. If everything looked alright, however, the matron of honour joined the right hands of the couple. Then they exchanged their vows of loyalty with the following words:

UBI TU GAIUS, EGO GAIA
(Where you are the husband, I am the wife)

And:

UBI TU GAIA, EGO GAIUS
(Where you are the wife, I am the husband)

The marriage ended with another sacrifice to the gods and prayers that the marriage should be a happy one.

In this scene the insides of a bull are being inspected.

A Roman bridegroom and his bride. Notice that their right hands are joined together. (Scene from a funeral altar)

A small figure of a leg offered to the god of healing, Aesculapius, in return for mending a broken leg. (Height – 22cm)

Illness

Most Romans knew very little about many aspects of health and medicine, although they were skilled in the use of herbs. When anyone fell ill or suffered an injury, the remedies were usually based on magic or superstition.

The Roman writer, Pliny the Elder, included the following cure for broken bones in his encyclopaedia of natural history:

A quick cure for broken bones is to apply the ashes of the jawbone of a boar or pig. You can also use boiled lard applied to the broken bone; this is a very quick cure. For fractured ribs, use goat's dung mixed with old wine.

Pliny *Natural History* 28.7.35

The Romans also made offerings to the god Aesculapius, god of medicine and healing, and asked for cures. This was one in a Greek inscription dating from the early Roman Empire:

The god replied that the blind soldier Valerius Aper should use the blood of a white cockerel mixed with honey as an ointment for his eyes. After three days he could see again.

A cured person often made an offering to the god in the form of the part of the body which had been cured. You may sometimes see the same kind of thing today in Catholic churches – 'votive offerings' in the form of parts of the body in gratitude for cures, or a ship in gratitude for rescue from shipwreck.

An offering of a pair of ears, suggesting that the owner had been cured of deafness

Death

Death and burial were also religious occasions. When a member of a Roman household died, it was necessary to make a sacrifice to the **lares** to purify the house, and nine days after the funeral a special sacrifice was made to the **manes** or departed spirits of the dead person.

Each year the *paterfamilias* carried out a strange ceremony called the **Lemuria.** Its purpose was to purify the house by persuading the spirits of the dead to leave the household and not haunt it. It took place on May 19th. The poet Ovid gives us this description:

At midnight the *paterfamilias* gets up. He makes a sign with his thumb in between his fingers in case he should happen to meet a spirit. He washes his hands in spring water and then takes some black beans which he immediately throws away, turning his face as he does so, and saying: 'I cast these away. With these beans I

restore me and my family.' He says this nine times, without looking back. People think the spirits gather the beans and follow behind the *paterfamilias* unseen. He puts his hands in water again and clashes sheets of bronze together. He asks the spirits to leave his house and says, nine times: 'Spirits of my ancestors, depart!' Then he looks back and is convinced that he has carried out the ritual correctly.

Ovid *Fasti* 5.419–444

QUESTIONS

1 What were the *lares*? Why did the Romans think it important to worship them? (page 7)

2 Who was the *paterfamilias*? What were his religious duties? (page 7)

3 Why was Vesta so important to the Romans? (page 7)

4 How did the Romans try to protect a mother and her new baby? Why was it necessary to do this? (page 9)

5 Who was the *Auspex*? Why did he inspect an animal's insides? (page 10)

6 What sort of cures did Pliny the elder recommend? Do you think they are based on magic or medicine? (page 11)

7 Why did the Romans carry out the *Lemuria*? What did the *paterfamilias* ask the spirits to do? (page 12)

THINGS TO DO

1 Compare modern ceremonies connected with birth, marriage and death, with the ones the Romans took part in.

2 Collect any remedies for illnesses which are based on magic and superstition. Try to answer the question: why do people still use them?

3 What celebrations have taken the place of the Roman religious ceremonies in the modern world?

This scene shows quite clearly the various parts of a Roman funeral procession. Try to pick out the widow of the dead man, the professional mourners, the horn and trumpet players and the flute players.

3: GODS AND GODDESSES

During the sixth century BC the Romans came into contact with two other peoples who lived in different parts of Italy – the Etruscans and the Greeks.

The Etruscans settled just across the river Tiber to the north of Rome and exerted great power over all the towns in the area, including Rome. They themselves had been in contact with Greek ideas and they introduced many of them into Roman religion. Their own religion was very mysterious and depended a great deal on the art of divination – that is, telling the will of the gods from signs or omens. These signs might be the size, shape and colour of an animal's internal organs, inspected after the animal had been sacrificed. The Romans were very quick to take up this idea as part of their own religion.

The Greeks, who had settled in southern Italy, had brought their own gods and goddesses with them from their native cities in Greece. The Greeks believed in the Twelve Olympians, six gods and six goddesses, who lived on Mount Olympus in Greece and directed all the affairs of the world. All kinds of legends and stories were told about them and the Greeks thought of them as superhuman beings who lived forever.

A statue of the Greek god, Apollo, which was made by the Etruscans and shows how the Etruscans saw the Greek gods which they had heard about.

Gods of trade, business and travel

By this time the Romans had given names and human shapes to many of their spirits and they began to think of them as being the same as the Greek gods and goddesses. The table shows the name of the Roman god or goddess, his or her Greek counter- part and his or her special powers. The Romans continued to believe in many gods and goddesses for most of their history, until Christianity taught them to believe only in one god. (See Chapter 6.)

Roman name	Greek name	Power	Symbol
JUPITER	ZEUS	King of the Gods	
NEPTUNE	POSEIDON	God of the Sea	
MARS	ARES	God of War	
APOLLO	APOLLO	God of the Sun and Prophecy	
VULCAN	HEPHAISTOS	God of Metalworking	
MERCURY	HERMES	God of Communications	

Roman name	Greek name	Power	Symbol
JUNO	HERA	Queen of the Gods	
MINERVA	ATHENE	Goddess of Science and Crafts	
DIANA	ARTEMIS	Goddess of the Moon and Hunting	
VENUS	APHRODITE	Goddess of Love	
VESTA	HESTIA	Goddess of Fire	
CERES	DEMETER	Goddess of Agriculture	

Jupiter, King of the Gods

He was originally the god of the sky and the weather. Because the sky and the weather were so important to farmers, it is easy to see why they thought Jupiter was king of the gods. He also had other names – Jupiter Lucetius, who controlled the daylight, Jupiter Fulgur, who sent the lightning and Jupiter Pluvius, who sent rainstorms.

Neptune, God of the Sea

Neptune was the Roman god of lakes and rivers until the sea-going Greeks introduced the Romans to the god Poseidon, god of the sea, and the two became one. He also caused earthquakes by banging his trident. He was greatly feared by the Romans, who knew about earthquakes from personal experience of eruptions of volcanoes like Mount Vesuvius and Mount Etna.

Mars, God of War

The Romans originally thought of Mars as a god of agriculture. When it became necessary to defend their land against enemies they made Mars a god of war.

Vulcan, God of Metalworking

Since the Romans were a practical people, it was natural for them to think of a god in the form of a blacksmith. They believed that he made thunderbolts for Jupiter under Mount Etna in Sicily. For this reason we call fiery and explosive mountains volcanoes.

Mercury, God of Communications

The Romans thought of Mercury first and foremost as the god who looked after trade and business. Many inscriptions have been found which praise Mercury for bringing large profits – an important part of Roman city life. The Romans thought of him as the same as the Greek god, Hermes, who was the messenger of Zeus and patron god of travellers and merchants.

Apollo, God of the Sun and Prophecy

Apollo was a Greek god whom the Romans worshipped directly. This is why there is no Roman name for him. As the god of prophecy, people believed he could answer questions about the future. The centre of his worship in Italy was the Greek town of Cumae on the Bay of Naples. People went there to consult him about their fate and fortune. The Romans also worshipped him as the Sun-god and called him Phoebus, which means 'shining'.

Juno, Queen of the Gods

Juno was the name the Romans gave to the spirit who looked after women. She was the wife of Jupiter and the Romans thought she was the same as the Greek Goddess, Hera, wife of Zeus and queen of the gods. One of her important tasks was to protect women in childbirth and because of this the Romans called her Juno Lucina.

Minerva, Goddess of Science and Crafts

She was an old Etruscan goddess of crafts and skills. The Greeks worshipped Athene as the goddess of wisdom and practical skill, and Minerva was thought of as the same goddess by the Romans.

Diana, Goddess of the Moon and Hunting

She was a country goddess of woods, women and childbirth. Later she was compared with Artemis, the Greek goddess of the moon and hunting, and became thought of as the same by the Romans. She had a sacred shrine on the Aventine Hill in Rome.

Venus, Goddess of Love

She was originally a country goddess of beauty but she became the Roman equivalent of Aphrodite, the Greek goddess of love. Roman legend tells of Venus as the mother of Aeneas, a hero from Troy, who sailed to Italy and founded a city which was to be the site of Rome.

Vesta, Goddess of Fire

She was a country goddess of fire and the hearth. The Romans always thought of her as a sacred flame, which they kept burning in a special temple in the centre of the city.

Ceres, Goddess of Agriculture

She was an early corn-goddess whom the Romans thought was the same as Demeter, the Greek goddess of corn and agriculture.

QUESTIONS

1 What was divination? How did the Romans learn about it? (page 14)

2 How did the Romans learn about Greek ideas? (page 14)

3 What effect did Greek religion have on the Romans? (pages 14 and 15)

4 Why were Neptune and Mercury important for the Romans? (pages 16 and 17)

5 What were Apollo's powers? Why do you think people worshipped him? (page 17)

6 Why do you think Vesta was so important to the Romans? (page 19)

THINGS TO DO

1 Find out more about Etruscan and Greek religion (see the booklist on p. 48) and try to discover other things that the Romans borrowed for their own religion.

2 Collect some stories about the Twelve Olympians.

4 Find out how many of the names of the gods and goddesses are used today for other purposes, e.g. advertising, space travel, science, etc.

Terracotta plaque of Ceres

4: PUBLIC WORSHIP

The twins Romulus and Remus as babies, with the wolf that suckled them. (About 3.5m long)

How religion first came to Ancient Rome

Roman legend tells the following story about the first king of Rome, Romulus, and his twin brother, Remus:

Having brought their followers together, they decided to found a city, but they could not decide which of them should be the founder. Romulus said: 'There's no need to fight about it; many people have great faith in the signs which the birds send; let us try the birds.' They agreed. Romulus made his way to the top of the Palatine Hill and Remus went to the Aventine Hill. Remus immediately saw six birds in flight, but Romulus saw twelve. They stuck to their agreement and Romulus was chosen to be the founder.

Ovid Fasti 4

Romulus was chosen because he had seen more birds than Remus and the people believed this was a sign that Romulus should be king.

Romulus then carried out a ceremony on a day specially chosen for the foundation of Rome. He prayed to Jupiter, Mars and Vesta, as he ploughed a furrow to mark out the boundary of the city. Jupiter answered with thunder and lightning in the left of the sky. They thought this was a good omen for the beginning of the new city.

Later, as the walls began to rise, Remus began to make fun of them for being so low and he jumped over them to show how easy it was for an enemy to do the same. Romulus immediately killed him, as an example to anyone else who might dare to do such a thing. He then went on to rule his city wisely for 38 years.

The second king of Rome was called Numa Pompilius. Later Romans believed that Numa was the first person to organize religious customs in a proper system of State religion by appointing priests and organizing public worship.

First of all he divided the year into twelve lunar months (*shorter than our calendar months*), and added extra months so that the full number of days in a year could be made up. Then he decided which days should be called 'lawful' and which should be called 'unlawful'. (No business could be carried out or contracts made on 'unlawful' days.) After that he appointed priests: one for Jupiter, one for Mars and one for an old country god called Quirinus. They were allowed to wear special robes so that people would recognise them. He also appointed priestesses to serve the goddess Vesta. He paid them grants from public money so that they could give all of their time to their duties. Finally he appointed a Chief Priest and gave him written instructions for all the rituals so that people might have someone to whom they could go with any problems to do with religious practice.

Livy *History of Rome* 1.19–20

Λ bust of Numa Pompilius

The next two kings were too busy with wars to spend time on improving the religious life of the city. The fifth king was an Etruscan called Tarquinius Priscus. During his reign the Romans began to study the flight of birds, because they believed that in this way they could find out more about the wishes of the gods. It was important to watch the way the birds flew, how many there were, where in the sky they were flying. Special officials (called **Augurs**) were appointed to study the movement of birds and explain what these movements meant.

The last king of Rome was an unpopular tyrant called Tarquin the Proud. There is a famous story about an incident that happened during his reign. An old prophetess, known as the **Sibyl,** travelled to Rome from the Greek town of Cumae with nine books of prophecies which she said had come from the god Apollo himself. Tarquin refused the price which she had asked for them. The *Sibyl* immediately threw three on to a nearby fire and demanded the same price for the remaining six. Again Tarquin refused. Again the *Sibyl* burnt three books and asked the same price for the remainder. Tarquin was now convinced that the books must be worth a great deal and so he bought them.

The **Sybilline Books,** as these books were called, contained much advice about religious matters and the Romans consulted them when things were going badly for the city. Sometimes the books suggested that the Romans should worship a new god. Many of these 'new gods' were originally Greek gods. This was how the worship of such Greek deities as Demeter, Hermes and Poseidon was brought to Rome.

An *Augur* in his official robes and carrying the *lituus* or sacred wand

The calendar of Numa Pompilius was the beginning of the official recording of all the religious festivals, phases of the moon, public holidays and all the other details which we expect to find in a modern calendar.

The calendar in the illustration shows the days of three months – April, May and June. The Roman week was eight days long and each day was given a letter from A to H. There was a market day, called **Nundinae,** on every eighth day. The calendar also gave information about individual days. For example, a day might be marked as follows:

N, which stands for Nefastus, and means a day unsuitable for business

F, which stands for Fastus, and means an ordinary working day

C, which stands for Comitialis and means a day for public meetings or assemblies.

Or it might be marked with the name of a religious festival. Three days in every month were especially connected with religious worship and were marked KAL (Kalends, 1st), NON (Nones, 5th or 7th), EID (Ides, 13th or 15th). They were also used as key days in reckoning dates.

Public calendars such as this were on display all over Rome, and individual families must have had private ones which included their own special celebrations.

Section of a Roman calendar. The festivals and key days are marked with the first three or four letters of their name, (EID − *Ides*).

	APRIL				MAY		
DAY	**DATE**	**TYPE OF DAY**	**FESTIVAL**	**DAY**	**DATE**	**TYPE OF DAY**	**FESTIVAL**
C	KALENDS	F	FESTIVAL FOR VENUS	A	KALENDS	F	GAMES FOR THE LARES AND THE
D	4	F					GOOD GODDESS
E	3	C		B	6	F	GAMES
F	DAY BEFORE	C	GAMES FOR THE GREAT GODDESS	C	5	C	· GAMES
G	NONES	N	PUBLIC FORTUNE	D	4	C	
H	8	N	HOLIDAY FOR CAESAR'S VICTORY	E	3	C	
			IN AFRICA	F	DAY BEFORE	C	
A	7	N	GAMES	G	NONES	N	
B	6	N	GAMES	H	8	F	
C	5	N	GAMES	A	7	N	LEMURIA
D	4	N	GAMES	B	6	C	
E	3	N	FESTIVAL FOR THE IDAEAN	C	5	N	LEMURIA
			MOTHER OF THE GODS	D	4	N	GAMES OF MARS IN THE CIRCUS
F	DAY BEFORE	N	GAMES FOR CERES	E	3	N	LEMURIA
G	(E)IDES	N	FESTIVAL FOR JUPITER VICTOR	F	DAY BEFORE	C	
H	18	N	GAMES	G	E(IDES)	N	FESTIVAL OF UNCONQUERED
A	17	N	FARMING FESTIVAL IN HONOUR				MARS AND OF MERCURY
			OF THE GOD, TELLUS	H	17	F	
B	16	N	GAMES	A	16	C	
C	15	N	GAMES	B	15	C	
D	14	N	GAMES	C	14	C	
E	13	N	FESTIVAL IN HONOUR OF CERES	D	13	C	

Here we see people taking part in the Lupercalia.

Important festivals in the Roman calendar

Here is a list of the main religious festivals held during the year by the Romans. Can you suggest reasons why these festivals were held at the times shown? And what kind of gods or spirits were worshipped during them?

January	**Compitalia** **Paganalia**	Marked the beginning of the ploughing season. Marked the end of the ploughing season. A pregnant sow was sacrificed to the earth god, Tellus.
February	**Lupercalia**	A fertility ceremony. Young men ran round the city striking women with strips of goat-skin to help them bear children.
March	**Fordicidia**	Cattle were sacrificed to Tellus to make sure that the earth would produce crops.
April	**Parilia**	In honour of an old country god, Pales. It also celebrated Rome's birthday. A procession was made round the fields.
May	**Ceremony of Puppets**	Straw puppets were thrown into the river Tiber. This was a substitute for human sacrifice, made in times of famine.
June	**Vestalia**	The storehouse of Vesta was cleaned and made ready for the grain of the new harvest.

July		Various agricultural festivals were held in honour of the gods of the countryside and harvest.
August	**Vinalia**	A lamb was sacrificed to make sure of a good vintage and the grapes of the new vintage were picked by the priest of Jupiter.
	Consualia	The first grain was burned in a special ceremony.
September	**No festivals**	
October	**Fontinalia**	Springs and wells were decorated with flowers to encourage the spirits of the waters.
	October Equus	The winning horse of a special chariot race was sacrificed and its head was cut off and fought for by two groups of men from different parts of the city.
November	**No festivals**	
December	**Saturnalia**	In honour of Saturn, who was the God of agriculture and father of Jupiter. This became a festival of great fun and gaiety when masters changed places with their slaves.

A priest making a sacrifice.

Temples for public worship

The Romans got the idea of building temples from the Etruscans. These temples were very similar to Greek temples and they were all built on the same kind of plan: a central, rectangular building (**cella**) to house the statue of the god, surrounded by a colonnade of marble columns supporting a sloping roof.

Roman temples usually stood on a high platform and could only be entered by means of steps at the front. The Romans thought of their temples as houses for the gods and goddesses. The statues inside were often decorated with presents of jewellery and precious ornaments given by worshippers. All sacrifices and prayers to the god, as well as processions, took place outside at a special altar.

Plan of a Roman temple

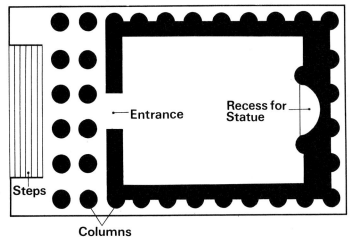

Steps

Entrance

Recess for Statue

Columns

right The temple of Jupiter in Rome (from a model)

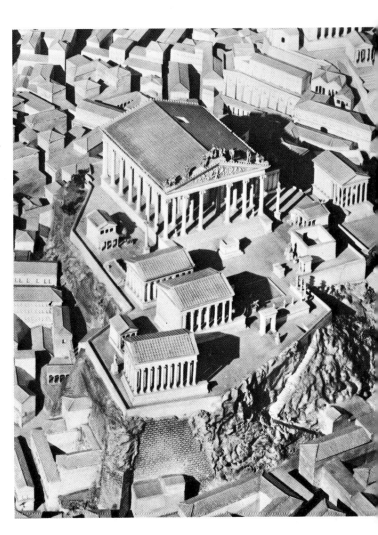

Here the *Haruspices* consult together after inspecting the insides of a sacrificed bull. They would then state the will of the gods from the shape and colour of the insides.

Priests

Nowadays we expect people who enter the church as priests or clergymen to study and to wish to serve God and humanity. We expect them to have a 'vocation' – a 'calling' by God to their task.

Roman priests were quite different. They were elected by the people and were officials of the State, just like civil servants or politicians. At the head of the system was the **Pontifex Maximus** — Chief Priest. Under him were various boards or committees of priests who looked after different departments of State worship. Certain gods and goddesses had special priests called **Flamens.** The **Flamen Dialis** was the priest of Jupiter, the **Flamen Martialis** was the priest of Mars. There were thirteen altogether. Then came the **Augurs** and **Haruspices,** who performed the same rituals as the **Auspices** (see page 10), and lastly the **Vestal Virgins,** who were priestesses of the goddess Vesta.

Table of priests

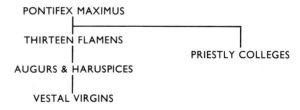

Terracotta plaque showing Vestals preparing to celebrate their festival to the Great Mother, Bona Dea, at which a pig was sacrificed.

Vestal Virgins

These were a group of six girls from noble families whose main duty was to look after the sacred flame of Vesta, goddess of fire. In a world where fire was important for heating, lighting and cooking, and where the fireplace was the centre of the household, it was only natural for the Romans to be very careful about protecting the sacred flame. If the flame did go out, it was difficult to relight it.

The flame was kept in a round temple in the Forum, and the Vestals lived in a special house built next to it. They entered the

The temple of Vesta in the Forum

goddess' service as early as the age of seven and stayed Vestals for thirty years, after which they could retire. While they served the goddess they were not allowed to marry. If one secretly did she was buried alive.

The Romans thought very highly of the *Vestal Virgins* and held them in great respect. Their work was important because people believed that, if the flame went out, great harm would come to the city. Apart from this special duty, they also took part in many festivals throughout the year.

Ceremony of a sacrifice

Here is a description of a sacrifice in connection with the dedication of a new Temple to Jupiter.

On June 21, under a clear sky, the whole area of the sacred precinct was surrounded by garlands of flowers. Soldiers entered the area with branches from lucky trees. Next the Vestal Virgins, together with young boys and girls whose parents were still alive, sprinkled the ground with water from springs and rivers. Then the Praetor (State Official), Helvidius Priscus, purified the area by sacrificing a pig, a sheep and a bull, and placing their entrails on a turf altar. Then he prayed to Jupiter, Juno and Minerva, and to all the other gods who protected the city, to support their work. He then touched the garlands that were wound round the foundation stone of the temple and woven around the ropes attached to it. At the same time all the people present dragged the huge stone to its proper place.

Tacitus *Histories* 4.13

There were three important rules for every ceremony. First, no foreigner was allowed to be present. This was to prevent any bad effect which a stranger might have on a private ritual. Second, no one was allowed to hear the most important parts of the prayers. This was because people believed that certain words had too much power to be spoken aloud. (Even today, parts of some Christian services are spoken very quietly so that the congregation cannot hear them.) Third, the ceremony had to be perfect in word and action. If a mistake was made, or somebody interrupted the priests, everything had to be done again.

This knife is the kind used for sacrifices. (Actual size)

QUESTIONS

1 Why did Romulus and Remus let the birds decide who should be the founder of Rome? (page 21)

2 What did Numa Pompilius do to organise a proper system of State Religion? (page 22)

3 Explain why the Sibyl's books were valuable for the Romans. (page 23)

4 How could the Romans tell what was due to happen on a particular day? (page 24)

5 Why do you think so many Roman festivals were connected with the countryside? (pages 26 and 27)

6 What went on at a sacrifice? Why were they held outside temples? (page 28)

7 Why were the Vestal Virgins so important for Roman religion? (page 30)

8 What were the rules that had to be followed for every ceremony? Why did the Romans take them so seriously? (page 31)

THINGS TO DO

1 Read Tacitus' description of a religious ceremony (page 31) and describe the scene as though you had been there.

2 Make a large Roman calendar for the classroom wall. Include all the festivals and make suitable drawings for each one.

3 Draw up a calendar of modern religious festivals and public holidays then compare this with the Roman calendar.

5: NEW IDEAS AND BELIEFS

Many Romans thought that the State religion did not really allow ordinary people to take part in the ceremonies or gain anything from them. The rituals were old-fashioned and often meaningless. Gradually many people lost interest and turned to other beliefs and religions.

Astrology

Astrologers believe that people's lives are affected by the stars and their positions in the sky. Many Romans believed that they could learn about the future by studying astrology, just as people today study their horoscopes in daily newspapers. In fact, as astrology became more popular, people began to consult the stars before doing anything important, in case it might turn out badly.

Working with someone's horoscope was very complicated and the astrologers who did it were known as **mathematici** – mathematicians. They were not popular with everyone. Tacitus, a Roman historian, writes:

Astrologers mislead powerful men and betray those with hopes. They are always being banned from Rome, but you will always find them there.

Tacitus *Histories* 1.22

Astrologers always made sure that their predictions were vague so that people could make them mean whatever they wanted. A modern horoscope is written in the same way so that it can refer to many people in different situations.

A zodiac, showing the various star-signs.

Philosophy – 'a love of wisdom'

Unlike many modern religions, the Roman State religion made very little attempt to teach people how to live. There were no examples to follow, no commandments to obey. There was nothing written down to help the ordinary person to cope with the day-to-day problems of life. Of course, many of the ordinary Romans were not interested in being told how to behave anyway – they thought they knew enough of life to know how to survive; that was all that was necessary. As long as the gods caused them no trouble and there was enough to eat, they had no worries. Serious thinking was a useless luxury.

Some of the more educated Romans thought differently. They felt it was important to think about the world and their place in it. But they found that the simple nature of Roman religion gave no help at all to those who wanted to improve themselves. To find solutions they began to study Greek philosophy. The word 'philosophy' means 'a love of wisdom'. In particular, there were two systems of philosophy which seemed to offer answers: **Stoicism** and **Epicureanism.**

A bronze skeleton. Some Romans kept these to make them think about death, and how short their lives were. (About 11cm long)

Stoicism

Stoicism was by far the more popular with the Romans because it told people what to do. The founder of the Stoics was a Greek called Zeno who began teaching in Athens in 301 B.C. He had no money to hire a lecture hall and so he taught in the famous painted colonnade, or **Stoa Poikile**, in the Athenian town centre. It was from this **stoa**, or colonnade, that the Stoics took their name. Stoicism was brought to Italy in the middle of the second century B.C.

Stoics believed that the universe was controlled by fixed laws which also controlled people's lives, and to go against them was the greatest sin. Everyone had to accept their position in life, and all men were brothers because they were ruled by the same laws. In the extract here a Roman Stoic, called Seneca, is writing to a friend of his about how he should treat slaves:

I'm pleased to hear that you live on good terms with your slaves. 'They are slaves' people say. No, they are men. 'They are slaves' people say. No, companions. 'They are slaves!' No, humble friends. 'They are slaves!' No, they are our fellow-slaves. Remember that fate has the same power over all men, slave and free. Remember that the man you call a slave is born just like you, lives under the same sky, breathes the same air, lives and dies, just like you do.

Seneca *Letters* 47

Because Stoicism tried to show men a better way of living, it was probably closer to what we call 'religion' than the old-fashioned ceremonies of the State religion.

This is a model of the kind of colonnade or *Stoa* that Greek philosophers like Zeno used to teach in.

Epicureanism

A different set of ideas was first taught by Epicurus in Athens in the first half of the second century B.C. The ideas were based on the theory that the world was made up of atoms – small particles that could not be destroyed. Epicurus taught people to aim for happiness and peace of mind. To do this he had to show them that everything they believed about death and the anger of the gods was just superstition. There was no life after death, he said, because when a person died every part of him was broken down into the original atoms; nothing was left. By stressing these ideas he tried to convince people that there was nothing to fear in life or death. He also tried to persuade people that they should avoid such things as politics, because they brought trouble and unhappiness.

Epicureanism was not as popular as Stoicism in Rome because many Romans were ambitious politicians who were keen to gain rewards both in this world and the next. A Roman poet, called Lucretius, explained the ideas of Epicurus in several books of poems which he called 'Nature of the Universe'. Lucretius did not believe in the religious ceremonies and sacrifices he saw in Rome as you can see from the extract here:

There is no true belief when people veil their heads, approach the altars, kneel before them and stretch out their hands to the shrines of the gods; when they kill animals and scatter the altars with blood; when they bind themselves with oaths. True belief is when someone can look at all the wonders of the world with a peaceful mind.

Lucretius *Nature of the Universe* 5.1198–1203

A bust of Epicurus

Religions from the East

Some Romans found answers to the problems of life in philosophy. Many Romans put their faith in gods and goddesses from Eastern countries like Egypt, modern Turkey, Asia Minor and Syria.

Statues of Isis and Serapis

Isis and Serapis

Isis was the greatest of the Egyptian goddesses and wife of the god, Osiris. In Egyptian legend, Osiris was killed by Set, god of the Underworld, who scattered his body throughout the land. Isis searched for the parts of Osiris' body and, when she had found them, was able to restore him to life. Out of this legend grew the worship of Isis and Serapis, who was thought to be the new Osiris restored to life.

Some people were attracted to worship Isis by processions such as the one described here:

Now the procession of Isis was moving by. Women in white dresses wore garlands of flowers and threw blossoms along the road where the procession would pass. Then came others carrying sacred emblems, followed by the sounds of flutes and pipes which made the sweetest music. Next came a chorus of noble young men dressed in white, chanting a beautiful song. Following them were the trumpeters of Serapis, playing his hymn. Then came the masses of followers of Isis – men and women of all ages and ranks. The women had their hair completely anointed with oil and covered with veils, but the men had completely shaven heads. They made a loud, jangling sound with bronze, silver and golden timbrels . . .

Apuleius *Metamorphoses* 9.9–11

At Rome the cult was banned for a long time until it was finally accepted as part of the State religion by the Emperor Caligula (A.D. 37–41).

Mithras

Mithras was a Persian god. He was originally worshipped as a soldier-god by the Persian nobles. For this reason he became very popular with the Roman Army, whose legions were stationed in all parts of the Mediterranean world.

Mithraism was a 'mystery' religion. The rituals were known only to his devoted followers. His temples were often located underground, in places rather like caves or crypts. His followers were 'baptised' into a brotherhood of worshippers. This was done in later Roman times by bathing the new recruit in the blood of a sacrificed bull. There were classes of followers, some known by animal names, such as Raven or Lion. All followers of Mithras had to live their lives according to strict rules, but we do not know what they were.

Mithras is usually shown in sculptures killing a large bull, from which many good things were believed to come. In this way his religion represented the victory of good over evil.

By the third century A.D., Mithraism had become almost the official religion of Rome. A famous French scholar has said that if something had happened to prevent the spread of Christianity, the western world would probably have been converted to Mithraism instead.

This carving shows Mithras killing the bull. Notice the signs of the Zodiac in the circle around Mithras. (About 3.5m high)

There were many reasons why these religions were so popular. First, they involved ordinary people in an active way. Second, the rituals were exciting, full of atmosphere and pageantry. Third, the ceremonies were secret and this made them more attractive. Fourth, some of the cults taught their followers a better way of life, something the State religion had never done. Last, these religions promised their followers a life after death, something which must have meant a lot to the ordinary Romans, whose day-to-day lives were often wretched.

Reconstruction of the inside of an underground temple built in London to Mithras

Emperor worship

The idea of worshipping a human being as a god is one which we cannot accept; neither could the Romans. But the peoples of the Eastern Empire had always thought of their rulers as descendants of the gods. It seemed quite natural for them to worship the Roman Emperor as a god. The first emperor, Augustus, was worshipped in this way:

Augustus allowed sacred areas to be dedicated to Rome and to his father, Julius Caesar, in Ephesus and Nicaea (places in Turkey). He instructed the Romans living there to worship them. But he allowed the native inhabitants of the cities to dedicate sacred areas to himself.

Cassius Dio *Roman History* 51.20

Augustus had to be very careful about allowing himself to be worshipped. Certainly he would have lost all his popularity at Rome if he had allowed such honours to be paid to him by Romans.

The emperor, Caligula, had completely different ideas. He set up a temple to himself as a god, with priests and sacrificial victims. In the temple stood a life-size statue of himself, in gold. Very rich people obtained the honour of being chief priest.

Suetonius *Life of Caligula* 22

No wonder he only survived for just four years before being killed by a soldier from his own bodyguard. By this time he thought that he was immortal and could not die; he thought wrongly!

Some of the emperors who followed him were made into gods after their death. Some took it seriously, others joked about it, like Vespasian (emperor A.D. 69–79) who said, as he lay dying, 'I think I'm becoming a god!'

An altar dedicated to the 'spirit' of Augustus. Romans were allowed to worship the *genius* or 'guardian spirit' of Augustus, but not the man himself.

An altar dedicated to Mars

Inscription

DEO
MARTI
BRACIACÆ
Q.SITTIVS
CAECILIAN
PRAEF.COH
I.AQVITANO
V S

Translation

to THE GOD
MARS
BRACIACA
by Quintus SITTIUS
CAECILIANus
PRAEFect of the COHort
no. I of the AQUITANians
IN PAYMENT of a VOW

Roman gods in Britain

The Roman Army played a great part in bringing local religions face to face with the State cult. In Britain, for example, the local gods were worshipped both by Britons and by the Roman soldiers. It was the custom to set up small altars, like the one in the photograph. Another altar (from Hadrian's Wall, in the north of England) has this inscription to a local British god:

This altar is dedicated to the god Cocidius by the soldiers of the Twentieth Legion, Valeria Victrix. They gladly and deservedly pay their vow.

Besides worshipping local gods, Roman soldiers brought the gods and religious beliefs from other countries as we can see from the altars and temples that they built.

Altars in honour of gods from other countries have also been found with inscriptions like the following that tell us the name of the god who was worshipped:

To the holy god Serapis, Claudius Hieronymus (an officer of the Sixth Legion) built this.

Five temples built in honour of Mithras have been found in Britain: three on Hadrian's Wall, one at Caernarvon and one in London. The foundations of the London temple are still to be seen in Queen Victoria Street.

The Romans also brought the worship of the emperor to Britain. At Colchester they built a temple to the Emperor Claudius, during whose reign the island was first successfully invaded and settled (A.D. 43–54).

QUESTIONS

1 What led some Romans to believe in astrology? Why were astrologers not always popular in Rome? (page 33)

2 Why did the more educated Romans find philosophy more helpful than religion? (page 34)

3 Why did Seneca show a kindly attitude towards his slaves? (page 35)

4 Why did Lucretius find it impossible to believe in the State religion? (page 36)

5 Why was the worship of Isis attractive to the Romans? (page 37)

6 Why was Mithras popular with the Romans? (page 38)

7 How was it possible for the Roman Emperors to be worshipped as gods? (page 40)

8 How did the worship of Roman gods and goddesses spread to other parts of the Empire? (page 41)

THINGS TO DO

1 Look at some modern horoscopes in popular papers and magazines and say how they can refer to many different people. Collect your own horoscopes and work out how often they are right.

2 Make a collection of the signs of the zodiac and write down the name of each sign e.g. Taurus=Bull and the times of the year for each.

3 Some modern religions are similar to the ancient mystery religions. Say which you think they are.

4 Read the description of the Isis procession (page 37) and write about it as though you had been there.

5 Try to visit a Roman site in Britain which is connected with religion e.g. Bath, where the Romans built a great temple and bath house to the goddess Sul Minerva; the Mithras temple in London; the castle at Colchester, which stands on the foundations of the Temple of Claudius; or Lullingstone villa in Kent, where the owners built an underground shrine to Christianity.

6: THE RISE OF CHRISTIANITY

In 40 B.C. the Roman poet, Virgil, wrote the following lines in one of his short poems:

The firstborn child of a new age is already descending from high heaven. With his birth the iron race will end and a golden race will arise throughout the world. Favour his arrival, goddess Lucina; your Apollo will reign at last.

Virgil *Pastoral Poems* 4

About forty years later, Christ was born in the Roman province of Judaea. Was it a remarkable coincidence or was Virgil giving a divine message to the world without his knowing it? We shall never know the answers to these questions, but even if one Roman had predicted the birth of Christ, the Romans themselves never gave Christianity a warm welcome until their empire had almost ceased to exist.

Jewish prisoners of war after the capture of Jerusalem in AD 71.
They are carrying the symbols of their religion – the seven-branch candlestick and the holy trumpets.

We do not know exactly when Christianity first came to Rome, but we do know that the Romans at first confused it with the Jewish religion. The Jews had been tolerated at Rome because they were ready to pray for the safety of the emperor, even if they did not believe in the State religion, and they caused no nuisance to the government. Virgil himself may have known about Jewish ideas and prophecies. Perhaps it was from these that he got the idea of a prophet to come.

By the time of the emperor Nero, who ruled at Rome from A.D. 54 to 68, Christianity was recognised as a separate religion and was very unpopular. In A.D. 64 there was a serious fire in Rome. Tacitus tells how the emperor punished the Christians because he wanted people to think they were to blame for the fire:

But no matter how hard he tried, he could not stop people thinking that he had ordered the fire to be started. In order to put an end to the gossip and suspicions, he laid the blame at the door of a group who were already hated for their evil practices – the Christians. Nero punished them with the worst tortures and cruelty he could think up.

Christus, from whom the group took its name, had been condemned to death and executed in the reign of the emperor Tiberius by the governor of Judaea, Pontius Pilate, and the evil superstition had been stopped for the moment. But now it was breaking out again, not only in Judaea, where the trouble had started, but also at Rome. It seems that all the dreadful and shameful things in the world come together and become popular in our city. Those who admitted they were Christians were arrested; what they told the authorities led to more arrests and convictions. All of them were charged but not so much because they were responsible for the fire, but because of their anti-social behaviour. Their executions were made laughable: they were covered in animal skins and torn to death by dogs, or were nailed to crosses and set alight when the evening came.

Tacitus *Annals* 15.54–4

Virgil

The fish, an early Christian secret symbol. The Greek word for fish IXTHUS contained the initial letters of the Greek words for Jesus Christ, Son of God, Saviour.

From what Tacitus wrote, it looks as if the Romans had completely misunderstood what the Christians did during their services and prayer meetings. First, they met together in private houses. To a Roman this could have looked like a secret plot against the emperor. Second, the Christians ate bread and drank wine together according to Christ's instructions:

He took some bread, gave thanks, broke it and gave it to them. He told them: 'This is my body, which I am giving for you; break the bread in memory of me.' And he did the same with the wine after supper: 'This wine represents the shedding of my blood, which is shed for you.'

Gospel according to St. Luke 22

From this the Romans decided that the Christians must be cannibals, eating 'body' and 'blood'. Third the Christians called each other 'brother' and 'sister', yet many were married to each other and such a marriage was forbidden in Roman law. Of course, the Christians used the words to remind themselves that all people were brothers and sisters in Christ's eyes. Lastly, the Christians said that 'God is love'. The Romans mistook this to mean that Christianity encouraged people to be too free and easy with their feelings and relationships. This was the 'anti-social' behaviour for which the early Christians were condemned. It was not long before the name of Christian itself was enough to place a person in danger.

A cross and an altar from a wall in Herculaneum, South Italy. The owner of the house kept these symbols of Christianity in an upstairs room, and to make sure they were not found, he used the altar as a chest and built a small cupboard around the cross to hide it. You can see where the cupboard used to be.

R O T A S
O P E R A
T E N E T
A R E P O
S A T O R

A word-square which hides the words PATERNOSTER twice. This is the beginning of the Lord's Prayer in Latin.

At the end of the first century A.D., Pliny, a Roman government official, was sent to the province of Bithynia on the Black Sea as a special representative of the Emperor Trajan. (Pliny was also the man who gave us an eye-witness account of the eruption of Mount Vesuvius in A.D. 79.)

One of the problems which faced him was that of the Christians. He wrote to the emperor for advice:

I usually refer to you, sir, all matters which I am not sure about. This is the case with the Christians. I have never taken part in any trials of Christians, so I do not know what offences are punished or investigated. I am not sure, for example, whether a man who repents should be pardoned for ceasing to be a Christian or punished for having been one.

I shall tell you what I have been doing in these cases. If any Christians are reported to me, I question them. If they believe, I question them again twice, reminding them of the punishment they will receive. Those who continue to believe, I execute, because I believe that their obstinacy should be punished. I have transferred others to Rome because, although they are equally mad, they are Roman citizens.

An anonymous pamphlet was published containing many names. I questioned them all. Those who denied the charge were ordered to offer prayers and wine to the gods and to your image, and to curse Christ, for I understand that no true Christian can be made to do this. I also tortured two female slaves, called deaconesses, but I found nothing but a wicked and evil superstition.

Pliny *Letters* 10.96

Trajan wrote back:

You have done the right thing. It is not possible to lay down a fixed rule. The Christians are not to be hunted out. If they are charged and found guilty, they must be punished, but not if they prove repentance by worshipping our gods. Then they must be pardoned. Do not pay any attention to anonymous accusations. This would be a dangerous example to follow and not in keeping with the times we live in.

Pliny *Letters* 10.97

Although Trajan's views may seem fairly tolerant, later emperors carried out many persecutions of the Christians. Finally in A.D. 311, the emperor Galerius passed a law which made Christianity a legal Roman religion. The following year the new emperor Constantine was converted to Christianity and in A.D. 313 he proclaimed that all Romans could worship whatever gods they wished. It was not until A.D. 395 that Christianity was made the official religion of the Roman empire. Fifteen years later the Goths over-ran Rome and the Empire began to collapse, but Christianity was strong enough to survive and to create a Holy Roman Empire. From these early beginnings Christianity has grown to become a world religion.

The Emperor
Trajan

48

QUESTIONS

1 How did Virgil seem to predict the birth of Christ? Why does he ask the goddess Lucina to favour the birth? (page 43)
2 What did the Romans think of the Jews? (page 44)
3 What calamity does Tacitus describe? Why did Nero blame the Christians, according to Tacitus? (page 44)
4 How did the Romans misunderstand what went on at Christian ceremonies? (page 45)
5 Why does Pliny have such a problem with the Christians? (page 46)
6 What kind of attitude does Trajan show towards the Christians in his reply to Pliny? (page 47)

BOOKS TO READ

Reference Books
Larousse Encyclopaedia of Mythology
Roman Mythology   Perowne   Hamlyn

Books for Younger Readers
The Romans and their Gods   Ogilvie   Chatto & Windus
Roman Mythology   Gilbert   Hamlyn

Others
The Religions of the Roman Empire   Ferguson   Thames & Huds

The fish design on the bottom of this small silver dish suggests that the dish may have been used in Christian ceremonies.